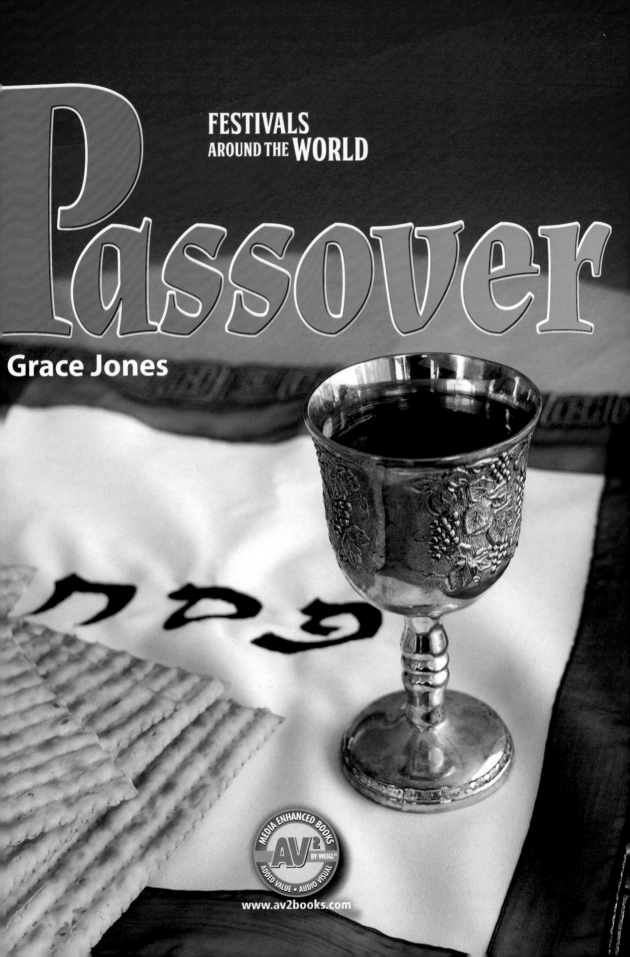

FESTIVALS
AROUND THE WORLD

Passover

Grace Jones

MEDIA ENHANCED BOOKS
AV²
BY WEIGL™
ADDED VALUE • AUDIO VISUAL

AV² provides enriched content that supplements and complements this book. Weigl's AV² books strive to create inspired learning and engage young minds in a total learning experience.

Your AV² Media Enhanced books come alive with...

Audio
Listen to sections of the book read aloud.

Key Words
Study vocabulary, and complete a matching word activity.

Video
Watch informative video clips.

Quizzes
Test your knowledge.

Go to **www.av2books.com**, and enter this book's unique code.

BOOK CODE

LBC67285

Embedded Weblinks
Gain additional information for research.

Slide Show
View images and captions, and prepare a presentation.

AV² by Weigl brings you media enhanced books that support active learning.

Try This!
Complete activities and hands-on experiments.

... and much, much more!

Published by AV² by Weigl
350 5th Avenue, 59th Floor New York, NY 10118
Website: www.av2books.com

Library of Congress Cataloging-in-Publication Data

Names: Jones, Grace, 1990- author.
Title: Passover / Grace Jones.
Description: New York, NY : AV2 by Weigl, [2018] I Series: Festivals around the world I Grades 4 to 6.
Identifiers: LCCN 2018003640 (print) I LCCN 2018004976 (ebook) I ISBN 9781489678157 (Multi User ebook) I ISBN 9781489678133 (hardcover : alk. paper) I ISBN 9781489678140 (softcover)
Subjects: LCSH: Passover--Juvenile literature.
Classification: LCC BM695.P3 (ebook) I LCC BM695.P3 J66 2018 (print) I DDC 296.4/37--dc23
LC record available at https://lccn.loc.gov/2018003640

Printed in the United States of America in Brainerd, Minnesota
1 2 3 4 5 6 7 8 9 0 22 21 20 19 18

032018
120417

Project Coordinator: Heather Kissock   Designer: Ana María Vidal

First published by Book Life in 2016

Weigl acknowledges Getty Images, Alamy, Bridgeman Picture Library, Shutterstock, and iStock as the primary image suppliers for this title.

FESTIVALS AROUND THE WORLD

Passover

Contents

Hello, my name is Jacob.

When you see Jacob, he will tell you how to say a word.

What Is a Festival?

A festival takes place when people come together to celebrate a special event or time of the year. Some festivals last for only one day and others can go on for many months.

Some people celebrate festivals by having a party with their family and friends. Others celebrate by holding special events, performing dances or playing music.

The word **rabbi** means "**teacher**" in Hebrew.

Jacob says:
SIN-A-GOG (Synagogue)
RAB-EYE (Rabbi)

What Is Judaism?

Judaism is a religion that began around four thousand years ago in the Middle East. Jewish people believe in one God who they pray to in a synagogue or a Jewish place of worship.

Jewish people read a holy book called the Torah. The Torah sets out God's laws which instruct people on how to practice their faith. A rabbi teaches Jewish people about God's word through the Torah.

What Is Passover?

Passover is a festival celebrated by Jewish people for seven or eight days in April every year.

Jewish people come together to celebrate a time in history when they were freed from slavery. They celebrate by having a special meal, cleaning their houses and telling each other stories.

Passover is also called **"Pesach."**

Jacob says:
PAY-SACK (Pesach)

9

The Story of Passover

A long, long time ago in Egypt, there was once a rich and powerful Pharaoh. The Pharaoh had many Jewish slaves, called Israelites. He treated them very unkindly. One day, a good-hearted man called Moses went to the Pharaoh and asked him to free the Israelites. The Pharaoh refused. Moses gave him a warning. "If you do not free them, God will send terrible plagues to Egypt."

Jacob says:
IS-RAIL-ITES (Israelites)
FAIR-OH (Pharaoh)

True to Moses'
word, ten horrible
plagues came
to Egypt. One
made painful
boils appear on
the skin of every
Egyptian. Another
sent millions of slimy
frogs across the land.

God's final plague was to kill
the eldest son in each house. Moses told
the Israelites to mark their doors with lamb's
blood so God would pass over their houses.
They did what Moses said and their sons
were safe from harm.

The final plague was so terrible that the
Pharaoh freed the Israelites. As they crossed
the desert they had only flat bread to eat
because they left in such a great hurry that
it did not have time to rise. The Israelites
celebrated. They were finally free.

Festival of Freedom

Jewish people celebrate Passover to remember the time when God "passed over" their houses and saved their eldest sons. This is why the festival is called Passover.

The festival also celebrates the Jewish people's faith in God and remembers a time in history when they became free.

Cleaning the House

Before Passover begins, Jewish people clean their houses. They search all over the house to get rid of any bread, cakes or biscuits.

Jewish people get rid of all leavened food, or food that has yeast in it. This is to remember the time when their people crossed the desert with only flat, unleavened bread to eat. If they find any, they put it in a bag and burn it.

Festive Food

On the first two nights of Passover, a special meal called the Seder is eaten with family and friends. Unleavened bread, called matzah, is made to remember the time when the Israelites crossed the desert with only flat bread to eat.

Three **matzah** are eaten at the Seder meal.

Bitter herbs, such as parsley, are eaten as part of the Seder meal. It is dipped in saltwater to remember the tears of the Jewish people when they were slaves in Egypt. This part of the meal is called the karpas.

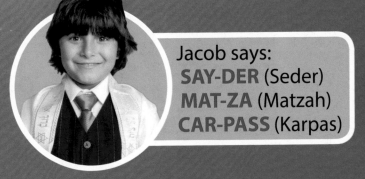

Jacob says:
SAY-DER (Seder)
MAT-ZA (Matzah)
CAR-PASS (Karpas)

The asking of questions at Passover is called the **Magid**.

The Seder

During the Seder meal, people read aloud from a Jewish book, called the Haggadah. The book tells the story of how the Jewish people escaped the Pharaoh and Egypt.

The youngest child at the table then asks their father four questions about the Seder. After the father finishes giving the answers, a cup of wine is drunk.

Jacob says:
HAG-A-DA (Haggadah)
MAG-ID (Magid)

Family and Games

During the Passover meal, three matzah are put on the Seder plate. A piece of the middle and biggest matzah is hidden somewhere in the house. The person who finds it wins a prize and shares it with their family.

Although Jewish people celebrate their faith in God during the festival, Passover is also about spending time with family, friends and loved ones.

Jacob Says . . .

HAGGADAH
HAG-A-DA
A book about the story of how the Jewish people escaped Egypt.

ISRAELITES
IS-RAIL-ITES
Jewish people born in Africa.

KARPAS
CAR-PASS
A part of the Seder meal where bitter herbs are eaten.

Magid
MAG-ID
The asking of four questions at the Seder.

Matzah
MAT-ZA
Unleavened bread eaten at the Seder meal.

Pesach
PAY-SACK
The name Jewish people call Passover.

Pharaoh
FAIR-OH
A great king of Egypt.

Rabbi
RAB-EYE
A teacher of the Jewish faith.

Seder
SAY-DER
A Jewish feast that takes
place during Passover.

Synagogue
SIN-A-GOG
A synagogue is
a Jewish place
of worship.

Log on to www.av2books.com

AV² by Weigl brings you media enhanced books that support active learning. Go to www.av2books.com, and enter the special code found on page 2 of this book. You will gain access to enriched and enhanced content that supplements and complements this book. Content includes video, audio, weblinks, quizzes, a slide show, and activities.

AV² Online Navigation

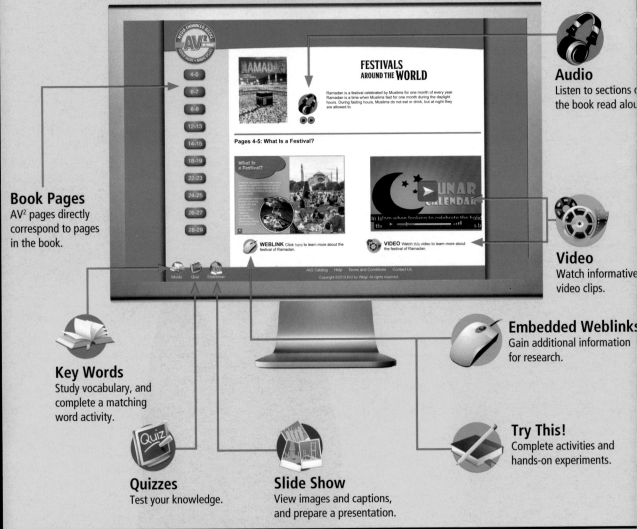

Book Pages
AV² pages directly correspond to pages in the book.

Key Words
Study vocabulary, and complete a matching word activity.

Quizzes
Test your knowledge.

Slide Show
View images and captions, and prepare a presentation.

Audio
Listen to sections o the book read alou

Video
Watch informative video clips.

Embedded Weblinks
Gain additional information for research.

Try This!
Complete activities and hands-on experiments.

AV² was built to bridge the gap between print and digital. We encourage you to tell us what you like and what you want to see in the future.

Sign up to be an AV² Ambassador at www.av2books.com/ambassador.